EASYWAY GUIDES

GUIDE
TO THE ROLE OF THE BEST
MAN

Anna Bennett

Easyway Guides
Brighton BN2 4EG

ISBN 1900694 04 2
ISBN 13: 9781900694049

Printed by Biddles Kings Lynn Norfolk

Cover design by Straightforward Graphics

Contents

Introduction

1. Marriage and Cohabitation   14

    Marriage   14
    Marriages must be voluntary   15
    Marriages which can be annulled   16
    Grounds for annulment   16
    Getting engaged to be married   17
    Marriage formalities   18
    Religious ceremonies   18
    Church of England-Licence to marry   19
    Publishing banns   19
    Common licence   20
    Special licence   20
    Superintendent registrars certificate   20
    Divorced persons wishing to marry   21
    Other denominations and religions   22
    Civil ceremonies   22
    Witnesses   23
    Marriages abroad   23
    Effects of a marriage   24
    Surnames   25
    Joint assets   25
    Common parenthood   25
    Marriages of convenience   25

2. The Role and Qualities of a Best Man   31

   At the reception   34
   The necessary qualities of a best man   35
   Well informed and briefed   35
   Level headed and punctual   36
   Stay sober   37
   Tact   37
   Speechmaker   37

3. Organising a Stag Party   39

   The party   39
   The stag guest list   39
   Letting other people organise the stag party 40
   The actual party   40
   Practical jokes   41
   Recording the party   41
   Making sure that the groom gets home   42

4. Making arrangements for the big day   44

   Assisting the bridegroom   45
   Working with future guests   45
   Order of service sheets   46
   Buttonholes and corsages   46
   Organising wedding clothes-what to wear   46
   Morning dress   47
   Lounge suits   47
   Buying or hiring a suit   48

Choosing the ushers/role of the ushers   49
Seating plan   51

5.   The day of the wedding   52

Morning   52
Ushers   53
Other   53
The ceremony   53
Anglican ceremonies   54
Buddhist ceremonies   58
Catholic weddings   59
Christian Scientist Church   61
Hindu ceremonies   61
Humanist weddings   62
Jewish weddings   63
Muslim weddings   64
Non-conformist weddings   65
Pagan ceremonies   66
Quaker weddings   67
Single-sex partnerships   68
Unitarian   69

6.   The reception   72

The seating arrangements   73
The seating plan   73
Wedding speeches   74
Cutting the cake   78
Display of gifts   78

Final duties   80

7. More on speechwriting and presentation   81

    Public speaking generally   81
    The person and the material   82
    Nerves   83
    Be prepared   84
    Structuring a speech   85
    Openings   87
    Introduction   88
    Closing   88
    Presentation skills   89
    Body language   89
    Vision   90
    Developing a style   90
    Use of language   92
    Using facial expressions   93
    Controlling movements   94
    Practicing presentations   95
    Developing voice   96

Appendix Wedding Planners   102
Useful addresses   110
Index

The Role The Best Man

Introduction

Most people who agree to be either best man and, more commonly nowadays, best woman, at a friends wedding, or a relatives wedding, are flattered and delighted to be able to fulfil that role. However, quite often when the reality sinks in a feeling of dread begins to manifest itself. As best man, you will, for quite a large proportion of the time, be the centre of attention. You will need to demonstrate organisation skills and also be able to stand up and deliver a speech, and a funny one at that. It is amazing how often it goes wrong. That is the reason for this guide.

The best man is the one who is level headed on the day of the wedding, carries an awful lot of responsibility, is a born after-dinner speaker, a diplomat and a trouble shooter. Sounds like a tall order doesn't it?

You have already taken the first step to becoming a successful best man by buying this guide. By following the advice within this book there is no reason why you shouldn't turn out to be a credit to the groom and bride and also feel proud of yourself.

One thing that is certain, most people don't have the first idea of the actual full ceremony of a wedding, the difference between a church wedding and a civil ceremony and the actual laws that govern weddings. In addition, since 2005, Civil Partnerships allow same sex couples to marry, albeit in a civil ceremony and not a religious ceremony. However, the role of best man is exactly the same in this situation.

The approach that this book takes, right at the outset, is to give some background in chapter one about the meaning of marriage and the laws underpinning marriage. Whereas most books dealing with the role of the best man ignore this aspect it is my view that a basic introduction to marriage is necessary and will help to raise the awareness of the best man to the particular context that he or she is operating within.

Throughout this book although the term 'best man' is used, it also pertains to best woman.

Good luck!

1

Marriage and Cohabitation

Although you are preparing for the role of best man, it is essential that you have some awareness of the institution of marriage.

The law of England states that marriage is the 'voluntary union for life of one man and one woman to the exclusion of all others'.

Much has changed in family life over the years and today, marriages break up with alarming frequency and more and more people choose to live together as opposed to marrying.

Before we discuss the preparations for getting married, which is the main aim of this book, we should look at the institution of marriage and how it works within the law. We will look at who can get married, the engagement, marriage formalities and the effects of marriage.

Marriage

The law states that, in order to marry, a person must:

a) be unmarried
b) be over the age of 18

You are also legally a single person if your previous marriage has been annulled. Basically, anyone who wants to marry must be a single person in the eyes of the law. A person must be over 18. If a person is aged between 16-18 parental consent must be gained. A marriage where one of the persons is under 16 is absolutely void. If someone marries between the ages of 16-18 the marriage is voidable as opposed to void (see below). Parents, guardians or the courts must consent to a marriage for someone between 16-18 years old.

No marriage can take place between close relations, i.e. blood relations, or non-blood relations where the relation is so close that a ban on intermarriage is still imposed. Adopted children are generally treated in law as blood relatives. Brothers-in-law and sisters-in-law can marry as can step-parent and stepchild if the stepchild has not been raised as a child of the family and is over 21 years old.

Marriages must be voluntary

A marriage must be voluntary and not brought about through coercion. This brings about a problem in law when arranged marriages take place, as is the custom in certain ethnic groups. In general the law does not interfere with arranged marriages.

However, the courts will get involved if it is felt that there is duress and there is a threat of injury to life or liberty or a child is threatened with expulsion from home or community.

Marriages which can be annulled

Void marriages

Certain marriages are regarded in law as void. This means that, in the eyes of the law the marriage has never taken place at all. Marriages are void where

- one of the parties is under 18
- the parties are closely related
- one of the parties is not a single person, i.e. the marriage is bigamous or polygamous.
- The parties are regarded in law as being of the same sex.

Certain marriages are regarded in law as valid until they are annulled. These are 'voidable' marriages and, in the eyes of the law can be annulled by either party.

Grounds for annulment

In order for a court to annul a voidable marriage the following grounds have to be demonstrated:

a) the marriage has not been consummated
b) the husband or wife had not understood the nature of the ceremony
c) the marriage was to someone of unsound mind
d) the marriage was to someone with venereal disease.

Getting engaged to be married

An engagement is not a precondition of marriage, as it once was. This is often the case, however. A couple will, after engagement, publicly announce their intention to be married. Legal disputes can, however, arise and couples can dispute ownership of property and gifts. An engagement ring is regarded as an outright gift in the eyes of the law.

If money has been expended on larger items, such as a house, in the anticipation of marriage, and the marriage has fallen through then this will become a legal dispute with each case turning on its own merit and the circumstances of any contract, written or unwritten. Certain insurance companies can offer insurance against weddings falling through or being cancelled. Cover can also be obtained for honeymoons falling through. If a couples wedding falls through they are legally obliged to return any wedding gifts received to their senders.

Marriage formalities

For a marriage to be valid, a formal licence and a formal ceremony are necessary. Authority to licence marriages is given to a priest of the Anglican Church and to civil officials (registrars). Every couple, therefore, must obtain permission to marry from an Anglican church or from a civil official. Many couples, because of cost, choose to marry in a registry office.

Religious ceremonies

Religious ceremonies are categorized according to whether they are solemnized by:

- The Anglican Church, including the Church of Wales
- Jews or Quakers (for whom special rules apply under the Marriage Act 1949)
- Some other recognized religion.

We have lived in a diverse ethnic society for many years and the rules governing marriage and religion are largely outmoded and in need of change. This will inevitably happen over time.

Church of England-licence to marry

About half of all religious marriage ceremonies take place in the Church of England. There are four ways to effect the necessary preliminaries for an Anglican marriage. Only one may be used. In order to obtain consent to marry in the Church of England you must either:

- publish banns

or obtain one of the following:

- a common ecclesiastical licence
- a 'special licence' also from the ecclesiastical authorities
- a superintendent registrars certificate from the civil authorities.

Publishing banns

The banns, or the names of the couple who intend to marry, have to be read aloud (published) in the church of the parish where the couple are resident. If the couple are resident in different parishes then the banns must be read in each parish church, in one or other of which the ceremony will take place. The priest needs seven days notice in writing from both parties before the banns can be read. The priest has to read them audibly in church on three successive Sundays. If there is no objection from any member of the congregation then, after the third reading the marriage can take place. If any objections are raised, and voiced audibly by a member of the congregation then the banns are void.

Common licence and special licence

This dispenses with the banns and is given by the Bishop of the diocese. You must make a sworn affidavit that there is no impediment to the marriage and that any necessary parental consent has been given and that you have resided in the parish for 15 days. Once granted, the licence to marry has immediate effect and is valid for three months. It will specify the church or chapel in which the marriage is to take place. The Special licence is issued by the Archbishop of Canterbury and enables a marriage to take place at any time or place. It also dispenses with the 15-day residence period. To get such a licence, which would for example be applicable if one of the parties was seriously ill, a sworn statement is required.

Superintendent registrars certificate

Although it is the norm for a marriage in the Church of England to take place after banns have been read, or after obtaining a licence from church authorities, an Anglican wedding can take place after a superintendent registrars certificate has been obtained. The parties must give notice to a superintendent registrar in the district in which they have resided for at least seven days before giving notice. They must make a solemn declaration that there are no lawful impediments to their union and that they meet the residential requirements. In the case of persons between 16-18, that they have parental consent. If the parties live in different districts then notice must be given in each district.

The notice is displayed in the superintendent's office for 21 days. At the end of that period, provided there are no objections, the certificate is issued. The marriage can take place in a church within the superintendent's district. The consent of the minister of the church must be obtained.

Divorced person wishing to marry in the Church of England

Where either party is a divorced person, a remarriage cannot be solemnized in the Church of England. This does not apply where the marriage has been annulled.

Other stipulations to a Church of England Wedding are laid down in the law, as follows:

- the marriage must be in an unlocked church
- between the hours of 8am and 8pm
- two witnesses must be present

Other denominations and religions

If you belong to another denomination or religion other than the Church of England, you must first obtain permission from the civil authorities to marry. There are four ways of meeting the legal requirements, of which only one need be used:

- a superintendent registrar's certificate
- a superintendent registrar's certificate with a licence. This has a residence requirement of 15 days.

For those seriously ill or detained, special provisions under the Marriage Act 1983 and the Marriage (Registrar General's Licence) Act 1970 will apply.

Weddings for Jews and Quakers can take place anywhere or at any time under the Marriage Act according to their own practices. The marriage is solemnized by a person designated for the purpose.

Civil ceremonies

The General Register Office will issue a form 357, which provides notes on the legal formalities of marrying. Marriages in a register office require a solemn declaration from both bride and groom according to the civil form:

- that they know of no impediment to their union
- that they can call upon those present as witnesses that they take each other as lawful wedded wife or husband.

The two witnesses present then sign the register. The superintendent registrar and the registrar must both be present at a civil wedding, which can only take place in a registry office, except in very unusual circumstances where people are ill or otherwise confined.

Witnesses

All marriages, without exception, be they religious or civil, require two witnesses to the ceremony. The witnesses need not know the couple. After a ceremony the witnesses sign the register and a marriage certificate is issued.

Marriages abroad

Generally speaking, a marriage that takes place in another country is recognised as valid in this country. However, all the laws associated with marriage in England and Wales must apply, such as the age restriction and the single person status. It is essential if a person intends to marry abroad that they seek legal advice in order to ascertain the status of the marriage in the UK.

Effects of a marriage

Being married confers a legal status on husband and wife. In general, questions of status, rights and duties concern the following:

Duty to live together

Husband and wife have a duty to live together. If one spouse leaves the other for good then an irretrievable breakdown has occurred.

Duty to maintain

Spouses have a duty to maintain one another. This extends to children, obviously, and becomes a particular problem on breakdown of marriage.

Sexual relationship

Husband and wife are expected to have sexual relations. Failure to consummate a marriage, as we have seen, can lead to annulment of a marriage.

Fidelity

Husband and wife are expected to be faithful to one another. Adultery is one of the main grounds for divorce.

Surnames

A wife can take her husband's surname but is not under a legal duty to do so. A wife's right to use the husbands surname will survive death and divorce. A husband can also take a wife's surname although this is unusual. Occasionally, couples will adopt both surnames. If a wife changes her surname to her husbands she can do so informally, simply by using the name. However, change of surname has to be declared to institutions such as banks and a marriage certificate has to be produced.

Joint assets

The matrimonial home as well as family income become assets of a marriage. A breakdown of marriage can lead to long and costly battles over assets of a marriage.

Common parenthood

Husband and wife automatically acquire parental responsibility for the children of their marriage. If the couple separate the courts can alter the relationship between parent and child.

Marital confidences

Secrets and other confidences of married life shared between husband and wife are protected by law. This is particularly relevant in this day and age where the tabloids invade the lives of people as never before. Married, and even divorced, persons can obtain injunctions to stop publication of confidential information.

Marriages of convenience

The laws surrounding such marriages have been gradually tightening up. Such marriages are seen as sham devices to get around UK immigration law. In order to issue a person with an entry clearance certificate to enter the UK as an affianced person or spouse, the immigration authorities will want to be sure that:

a) the 'primary' purpose is to get married and that a separation will not take place after marriage and entry
b) that spouses intend to live together as husband and wife
c) if the couple are not already married that the marriage will take place within six months.

It also has to be shown that parties to the marriage will settle in the UK.

Having discussed the basic laws surrounding marriage it is now time to concentrate more fully on the role of the best man at a wedding.

The Role of The Best Man

The Best Man

The Role of The Best Man

2

The Role and Qualities of a Best Man

A wedding is a well organised event and it is the role of the best man to ensure that proceedings go smoothly. A best man's role is many and varied. The groom has to be at the ceremony on time, one of the most important roles. Guests have to be seated correctly and also, after the actual wedding have to be transported to the reception.

At the actual reception, the focus is on the best man and his or her speech. It is the one that guests want to hear. A best man's speech is very important as this can make the occasion or can leave it flat. There are key tips on speech writing and presentation in the final chapter of this book.

The main roles of the best man are as follows:

- Organising the stag party for the groom
- Ensuring the groom gets to the ceremony
- Acting as witness at the wedding
- Organising wedding photo groups
- Assisting guests in their journey to the reception
- Making the main speech at the reception.

31

It is very important that the best man plans ahead as there are a lot of things to cover. Whilst not everything is the responsibility of the best man, overall the responsibility falls on your shoulders!

As with everything, a well laid out plan, put together as far in advance as possible, will prove to be a great help. Below is an example of a plan which will also show you the key times in which to do things.

1. Receive invitation to be best man	Can happen up to 2 years in advance but say within 1 year period.
2. Work with groom in choosing ushers	6 months before wedding
3. Start organising the stag party	3 months before
4. Review wedding plans with bride and groom go with groom to get fitted with suits etc.	3 months before
5. Finalise plans for stag party start work on speech	2 months before

6. The stag party happens!	1 month before wedding. Never night before.
7. Meet ushers, discuss duties, check groom has ring, finalise speech.	2 weeks before the wedding.
8. Wedding rehearsal happens, finalise wedding schedule, hire suits and finalise speech	1 week before wedding.
9. Last minute checks of everything!	1 night before wedding.

The above is a basic guide. It is up to you how you plan but, importantly, do plan. There is an ideal plan set out in the appendix to this book. Essentially, the most important role of the best man is to help the groom. The best man will get involved in the wedding preparations, help choose clothes and any other accessories, arrange transport, collect the buttonholes, help choose the ushers. The best man will also organise the stag party and make sure that the groom survives the party and gets home afterwards.

On the wedding day itself, the best man should remain calm. Other people, especially relatives, will not be calm. On the morning of the wedding the groom must be correctly dressed and arrives at the church on time with all the relevant documents and the ring. The best man will look after the ring until it is used in the ceremony.

When at the church, the best man will stay at the grooms side, standing a little behind and to the right of him during the ceremony, so that rings can be handed over. The best man will escort the chief bridesmaid into the vestry to sign the register and will escort her out of the church after the service. The best man will also be responsible for making sure that all fees are paid.

Once outside the church, the best man will assist the photographer, making sure that everyone is in the right place at the right time when the photographs are taken. After the photographs, videos and whatever else is happening to ensure that a record of the wedding is in place, the best man will ensure that everyone is sent on their way to the reception, that transport is in place and so on.

At the reception

At the reception, if there is one, the best man may be asked to announce the guests as they approach the receiving line. He or she can generally help to ensure that everything is running smoothly by playing host, offering drinks, chatting to people, helping to make them comfortable, making introductions and helping people to their seats. This particular role, that of host, is very important because at weddings, especially where people don't know each other, some people may feel uncomfortable. A wedding is an ideal forum for, on one hand, big ego's to show off and play to the gallery and on the other for the less confident to feel a little scared of the whole occasion. This is where the qualities of the best man can be most needed.

The best man will usually introduce the first speaker, responds to the toast from the bridesmaids, gives a speech of his own and then reads out the congratulatory messages from people who have been unable to attend. He will dance with the chief bridesmaid and the bride and as many other of the female guests as possible.

Finally, when the married couple are leaving for their honeymoon, the best man will make sure that the car is at the door waiting to take them away, packed with their luggage and with all necessary documents in place.

The necessary qualities of a best man

The 'best' best man will be self motivated and able to take the initiative and shoulder responsibility. Not many of us have all the qualities necessary to be a best man. However, it is important to raise awareness of the main qualities needed in order to ensure that the role is fulfilled and that the day goes off smoothly.

Well informed and briefed

During the period running up to the wedding, a lot will be happening and it is up to the best man to be as well informed as possible. There will be many things to achieve and many questions to answer. It is of vital importance that the best man knows the format of the day and where everyone should be at a particular time.

Regardless of how organised you are as a person, it will be necessary to plan using a personal organiser. Make sure that you have all aspects covered and that they are laid out on a weekly and monthly basis. As the wedding gets closer then they will become daily tasks. See appendix for a model organiser.

Level headed and punctual

It goes without saying that a best man, having so much responsibility to ensure others enjoy the day and that everything works like clockwork, should be level headed, calm in a crisis and punctual. Given that co-ordination is so important on the day, it is no good having as a best man someone who is hopelessly unpunctual.

Everything should be checked in advance to ensure that no obstacles are put in the way of smooth co-ordination. Everything is timed in advance, or should be. Almost military precision may be needed on a wedding day.

Stay sober

Again, if the best man is responsible for ensuring that a wedding day goes off successfully, then it is no good drinking large quantities of alcohol to give Dutch courage. This can detract from the proceedings as people can detect very easily when a person has had too much to drink. It doesn't exactly engender confidence.

Tact

Tact is a crucial quality of a best man. Tact usually increases with a persons level of maturity. It is important to notice and deal with problems before they arrive. Problems can be anything from family arguments to people sitting alone, to the drunken buffoon annoying others.

Speechmaker

This is one of the most important elements of the best

man's duties. Making a speech may be a good idea one year before the wedding but on the actual day it can be nerve wracking. We will be covering speeches in more depth later. The speech shouldn't go on for ever. It should be around four to five minutes long and no longer. It is almost certain that the speech will be well received as everyone will be in a good mood. However, don't try to be too clever, don't attack people and be sincere and to the point. The best speeches are mainly the shorter ones and are not too difficult to put together and deliver.

Overall, preparation is the key to ensuring that your performance as best man goes off without a hitch. The following chapters will help to ensure that this will be the case.

3

Organising a Stag Party

Before we discuss the details of planning the wedding we will discuss the planning and execution (unfortunate phrase!) of the stag party.

The party

This entails ensuring that the party itself is organised. As we will see, this can range from a basic night at the pub to something far more elaborate, such as a weekend away in a European city, such as Amsterdam or Paris.

It goes without saying that the more elaborate and complex the party the more responsibility that will fall on the best man. Trips away mean flights and hotels and nightclubs or other venues to book.

The stag guest list

This can be a tricky part of the whole operation. As far as possible, guests should be chosen for their ability to get on with others. A drunken night out can end in fisticuffs if the wrong people are invited. Usually 20 is the maximum and a lot of thought should be given as to whom. In addition to the profile of the list, thought needs to be given as to whether all people can fit in comfortably with the plans. For example, if the groom has decided to travel abroad, can everyone afford it? This is an important consideration and should be discussed with guests, or potential guests, before issuing invites.

Letting other people organise the stag party

It could be that if enough money is available and the organising is seen as a headache, then employing a company to organise the party is the best option. There are numerous companies available in the U.K who will organise a stag do and the types and kinds of events that they will organise, from a weekend away to mountain climbing, are numerous. See the appendix for a list of companies, websites and phone numbers.

The actual party

As we have seen, the best man ideally is a person who is highly organised. These organisational skills can be put to the test on the day of the stag party.

Getting everyone together at the initial place of meeting is a key task at the outset. Making sure introductions are made is also very important. It is amazing how many people wander around without knowing each other during the course of a stag night. This is down to weak social skills of organisers.

Make sure that the place to meet is pleasant and that people can settle in. Avoid places like railway station pubs. Try for more city centre or town centre venues. If the trip is abroad then make sure everyone meets in a hotel lounge or somewhere similar. Go easy on the boozing before arriving at the destination as this can jeopardise the party.

Managing the drinking during the party is also important. People drink at different speeds and therefore will be buying drinks at a different speed. Either a kitty system should be organised or people pay for their own in small groups. A minor point but an important one.

Practical jokes

Practical jokes at the grooms expense are a feature of any stag night. Basically, a little gentle humiliation is in order. Don't take the practical jokes too far however, as this can cause offence. One of the least harmful ways is to spring a surprise such as a strip-o gram (if the audience is male or the opposite if it is female).

Recording the party

Make sure that a photographic or video record is

available of a stag party. This party is very important and likely to be remembered, so it is important to have an adequate record which can be saved for posterity, in much the same way as the actual wedding day.

Making sure that the groom gets home

One of the most important tasks of the whole night is making sure that the groom survives without major trauma, such as fighting or being thrown into prison. Keep an eye on the groom and ensure that at the end of the night wherever you may be, he is tucked up safely in bed with no damage done!

The Wedding day

4

The Wedding- Making Arrangements for the Big Day

As with all planning, the longer in which to do it the better. This chapter goes through all the key areas that will need to be planned plus will act as an aide-memoir to help you stay organised.

On receiving your own personal invitation to the wedding you should reply immediately and ensure that you have that date firmly in your diary. If you have a partner that person will also be invited. However, if you don't have a partner then it is unwise to bring a stranger with you.

The best man will always buy the prospective bride and groom a gift. It is probably better to choose this off the wedding list. You will get information about the list from the bride, who will either be managing this herself or a store will be managing it.

Assisting the bridegroom

The best man will usually support the groom during the planning stages of the wedding. It is important to keep up-to-date with the different stages so that you can be of practical help.

Accompanying the groom to choose clothes and accessories, helping with planning the honeymoon details, arranging documents, these are all invaluable areas where you can be of use. Other areas are ensuring that the paperwork has been completed for the actual wedding, such as the banns, and that the ring has been purchased.

Working with future guests

On the actual wedding day, the best man will have a lot to do with the guests. However, even at this early stage you may get involved. For example, you may get involved in helping to book hotels, advise on gifts, advise on the best route to get to the wedding and so on. It is important to visit the reception venue with the bride and groom several months before the wedding. The little details can be checked at this stage, such as parking, whether there is to be a toastmaster and when the guests should leave. The bride and groom will also need to book a room where they can change into their going-away clothes after the wedding.

Order of service sheets

These are printed sheets so that guests can follow the service without referring back and forth from prayer book to hymn book. These should be collected in advance from the bride and given to the chief usher. They will then be given to guests by one of the ushers as they enter the church.

Buttonholes and corsages

The groom traditionally pays for the buttonholes for himself, the best man and the ushers. Normally, the principal men wear white carnations, and the bride and groom's mothers have small corsages of flowers to match their individual outfits. These are usually delivered to the bride's parents home on the morning of the wedding, along with the bouquets.

It will usually be the responsibility of the best man to ensure that the groom, the ushers and the groom's parents all have their flowers.

Organising wedding clothes-what to wear

Weddings differ and so do the clothes that people wear. You will know the clothes that will be required following your discussions with the bride an groom. For most weddings there are two main options, either morning dress or a lounge suit. Whatever the bride has chosen, all the men in the wedding party, the principal men, will wear the same style. If you are wearing a lounge suit then you will be expected to foot the bill. If morning suits, then these are usually paid for by the bride's family. You will pay for your own shoes and accessories.

Morning dress

Where the wedding is a formal affair, the bride will usually ask the men in the party to wear grey morning suits. These suits comprise a grey suit with tail coat, grey top hat and gloves and usually a white shirt. Socks and shoes are usually black. The tie or cravat should never be black. Alternatively, the bride may choose a black tail coat for the men along with pinstripe trousers. Again, you would wear matching black socks and shoes and a tie (not black).

Lounge suits

If the wedding is less formal (and most are) then the bride will normally prefer the men to wear a lounge suit. The choice of style and colours should be decided by the groom. It is important to check with the bride as to the overall colour scheme, which includes flowers and dresses. This will affect the colour of the lounge suits.

Buying or hiring a suit

The difference here is based on how much for the item of clothing and how often will you use it. For a formal suit it is almost certain that this would be used once every blue moon so it is safe to hire one as opposed to wasting money buying one. If you are wearing a lounge suit however, it is usual to buy one off the peg (or get it tailored if you have the money). In either case, it is a good idea to ensure that you know what you are going to wear, what the bride would like you to wear and what the groom has chosen. Complete your ensemble with a matching shirt and accessories.

If a morning suit is required, and the best man is only destined to wear it on one occasion, then hiring it is the best answer. If all the principal men are hiring their suits then you may well be invited along to the fitting. If you are not included in this then you should choose a reputable firm to go and book your suit for the day. An obvious one that springs to mind is Moss Bros.

It is important that the suit fits well and that you feel comfortable as it will be a long day and you also want to look and feel good as you will be the centre of attention. A dress rehearsal with the groom several weeks before the wedding is always a good idea, to iron out any last minute problems.

Choosing the ushers-role of the ushers

The best man is in charge of the ushers. It will be up to the best man to ensure that they know their duties and are properly dressed and in the right place at the right time.

The groom will choose the ushers and will usually include close relatives such as brothers, cousins etc. Normally there are four ushers and they will get together with groom and best man several months before the wedding to discuss the role and to introduce each other if appropriate.

This will be the occasion to ensure that the ushers know what type of clothing they should wear and also to go through the whole wedding day with them making sure that they are thoroughly briefed.

The person selected as chief usher will take charge of buttonholes and order of service sheets at the church, collecting them from the bride or best man before the ceremony.

The ushers will be the first to arrive at the church, usually about an hour before the ceremony. They will distribute buttonholes and direct the guests to the correct place. They will also discourage the use of cameras if this is not allowed in the church (if the ceremony is in a church).

As guests arrive at the ceremony, one of the ushers will hand order-of-service sheets or hymn and prayer books, asking if they are friends of the bride or groom. If the occasion is formal the usher would offer a female guest his arm and escort her to her seat on the left hand side of the church if she is a friend of the bride and the right hand if she is a friend of the groom. Her partner and any children would follow behind.

If two single female guests arrive together then the usher would escort one after the other, usually eldest first to their seats. At a less formal wedding the usher would simply direct guests to their seats.

The groom's parents will sit in the second pew from the front on the right hand side. If there are any divorced parents in the family, the ushers should be forewarned and be ready to explain the appropriate seating arrangements. Usually, if the parents are divorced but not remarried then they would sit together. If they are remarried then the mother would sit in the first pew with her husband and the father in the second pew. The last guest to arrive is the bride's mother who will be escorted to her seat by the chief usher. She will be seated in the front pew on the left side of the aisle, leaving one seat on the right for her husband, when he has 'given away' his daughter, the bride. The ushers will seat themselves at the back of the church so that they can deal conveniently with latecomers to the ceremony.

Seating plan

The plan below represents the ideal seating for a formal wedding.

BRIDE'S PARENTS	AISLE	GROOM BEST MAN
GRANDPARENTS BROTHERS AND SISTERS		GROOM'S PARENTS
OTHER RELATIONS OF THE BRIDE		GRANDPARENTS BROTHERS AND SISTERS
BRIDES FRIENDS		OTHER RELATIONS OF THE GROOM
USHERS		GROOM'S FRIENDS
		USHERS

After the ceremony has finished, the ushers will move people out to the correct places for the photographs, arrange transport and direct people to the reception. At the reception, the ushers may be asked to help in offering drinks to guests as they arrive, introduce people to one another as appropriate and dance with as many partners as possible.

5

The Day of the Wedding

Morning

The morning of the actual wedding is a very busy time for the best man. There is an awful lot to remember and the best mans planner at the rear of this book will prove invaluable.

Around a week before the actual wedding, you should check up on what is outstanding, or what is left to do. Many tasks will have been completed before the wedding, so the remaining tasks will need to be memorised.

On the morning of the wedding, it is important to phone the groom to ensure that he is up, has all the proper clothes and is ready and set to go. Check that all the documents and the ring are in his possession. He will need the certificate of banns from the church or the marriage licence, money for church or other fees, passport and tickets for the honeymoon, car keys and any other document or item relevant to the wedding.

If his vehicle is to be parked at the reception site in the morning, ready for the couple's getaway then he will need reminding that you will be driving it there and ensure that all luggage is in the car.

Finally, remind him what time you will returning to collect him for the ceremony.

Ushers

Check that the ushers know what time they should arrive at the church and that they know the location. Check that the clothes and the cars are ready. Ensure that the chief usher has the order of service sheets with him. These will either have been delivered to him beforehand or should be collected from the bride.

Also check whether he has the buttonholes for the wedding.

Other

Remind the bride's father to bring any telemessages or other messages. Also check that the brides honeymoon case and going away outfit is at the reception venue.

The ceremony

In all cases of church weddings, the minister will issue

instructions to all and sundry, so, ultimately there is no real need to worry. The two main duties of the best man are to get the groom to the church on time (not a good idea to have a stag night the day before the wedding) and to take charge of the rings.

Below is a brief outline of the different types of ceremony, covering a number of religions including Catholic, Jewish and non-conformist weddings.

Anglican Ceremonies

In Anglican faith, the ushers will be the first to arrive at the church. They will know how to seat the guests and have enough orders of service and prayer/hymn books for everyone. In short, their role is that of organising the basics, to ensure that the ceremony gets off to a good start.

Seating is arranged so that in the front pew, on the right hand side sits the groom and best man, with the grooms family seated alongside and immediately behind. The front pew on the left is reserved for the family of the bride and the bride's attendants. The guests will arrive 15 minutes before the service and they will be seated by the ushers-bride's family to the left and groom's to the right.

Close family of both bride and groom are seated at the front with guests seated appropriately from front to back.

After the ushers, the bridesmaids and bride's mother will arrive. After this, the bride will arrive led in by her father. The bridesmaids will assist the bride to make sure that her gown and veil are neatly arranged and secure. They will then take their places behind her, in pairs with the youngest first, and begin to walk up the aisle. As the bride and father enter the church they should give one of the ushers a signal to inform the minister or priest that they are ready.

At this signal, the organist will begin to play the chosen music and the groom and best man will leave their seats to stand in front of the chancel steps waiting for the bride and her father.

On arrival at the chancel steps the bride will release her father's arm and the groom will stand on her right hand side with the father just behind the bride. The best man stands on the groom's right. The bride will hand her flowers and any other items to the chief bridesmaid or matron-of-honour so that her hands are free for the ceremony. If there are no attendants she will hand these things to parents or friends.

The minister or priest will begin the ceremony with a short address, reminding the congregation of the solemnity of the occasion and that it is a happy event for the families and for the couple. Guests will be guided by their order of service.

The priest/minister will ask bride and groom separately whether they will take each other as spouse, then will say 'who gives this woman to be married to this man?'. The bride's father will step forward saying 'I do' and will take her right hand in his and place it palm down in the minister's hand.

The minister then places her hand in the groom's right hand and the symbolic gesture of giving away the bride is then complete.

With prior arrangement with the minister or priest this part of the service can be omitted as it is seen as old fashioned and irrelevant. It may also be that the bride has no one to stand with her in her father's role.

The bride and groom now exchange vows and give rings. The best man will place the ring on the minister's prayer book. After the exchange of vows and rings the couple are declared husband and wife and are invited to kiss to seal the ceremony.

At this point, the bride's father will take his seat with the bride's mother in the front pew, likewise the best man will take his seat. The couple will now kneel at the chancel steps to take the blessing and after prayers the minister or priest will lead them to the altar. If there is to be a communion it will be made at this point.

After this ceremony, the newly married couple, their parents, the chief bridesmaid or matron of honour and the best man now go into the vestry with the minister to sign the marriage register. The completed certificate is given to the couple. The organist will then perform for the congregation.

Leaving the church

The procession will form behind the couple as they walk down the aisle. If there is a flower girl she will walk in front of the bride scattering petals as she goes. The pageboy and ring bearer (if any) will follow the bride and groom carrying the train followed by the best man and chief bridesmaid or matron of honour, then ushers paired with bridesmaids. The bride's mother walks with the groom's father and the groom's mother walks with the bride's father as they follow the attendants. As they are walking friends and family will follow in sequence from the front pews onwards.

If it has been agreed, the photographer or video crew can take photos and videos but this is usually not permitted within the church. After the ceremony the photographer will arrange guests for group pictures, with the help of the ushers, and take individual and joint shots of bride and groom. Group shots are then taken.

Blessing services

For those who have been divorced or are marrying for a second time and wish to have an Anglican service to celebrate the wedding in a church where the vicar will not solemnize the wedding, a service of blessing is an alternative option.

In such a service, the couple will walk down the aisle together at the beginning, or if she has not been married before, the bride may be escorted to join the groom who is waiting at the altar, while the congregation are singing the first hymn. The couple will then make their promises in front of the congregation as they have already done at the previous civil ceremony.

Buddhist Weddings

Weddings under the Buddhist faith are very rare as there is no prescribed wedding ceremony. It is possible to devise an individual civil ceremony reflecting the couple's cultural traditions and for a Buddhist priest to undertake a blessing.

Catholic Weddings

Any marriages undertaken outside of the Church of England will require a licence. A couple must give notice of their intention to marry to a local superintendent registrar. The marriage itself can be authorised by a priest. If this is not the case then a registrar must be present.

If a couple want to marry in a Catholic Church they will have to visit the priest and discuss the intended wedding. In relation to the actual ceremony, if the marriage is between a non-Catholic and a Catholic then the mechanics of where to get married and who attends to give blessing will need to be discussed.

If both parties are Roman Catholic, the wedding ceremony will usually form part of a full nuptial mass. The main elements of the service will cover the significance of marriage, a declaration that there are no lawful reasons why the couple should not marry, promises of faithfulness to each other and the acceptance to bring up children within the Roman Catholic faith.

The service begins with a hymn and a bible reading, followed by a sermon. The priest will then ask if there is any impediment to a marriage and calls on the couple to give their consent 'according to the rite of our holy mother the church' to which each person responds 'I will'. The couple join right hands and call upon the congregation to witness the marriage and then make their vows to cherish one another. Vows are then exchanged, the priest will confirm them in marriage and the best man hands over the ring which is blessed and given or exchanged, with the couple acknowledging them as a token of their love and fidelity. In addition to the ring, the groom gives gold and silver to the bride as a token of his worldly goods. Once the rings are blessed, the groom places the ring first on the thumb of the bride and then on three fingers in turn. Prayers and nuptial blessings follow.

After the final blessing is the dismissal, whereupon the bride, groom and bridal party move into the sacristy to make the civil declaration and to sign and witness the register. If there is to be a nuptial mass the bridesmaids take their seats in the front pew.

For the nuptial mass, the couple return to the sanctuary. They then kneel and the bride is assisted by the groom. If Holy Communion is to be received, those taking it move forward at the appropriate time, returning to their pews afterwards. When the mass comes to an end, the couple proceed down the aisle from the sanctuary, followed by the chief bridesmaid and best man, and then the other bridesmaids, pageboys and parents before the rest of the guests.

Christian Scientist Church

If the minister of the Christian Scientist Church has registered with the appropriate local authority then the Church is licensed for marriage ceremonies. However, as the minister of the church is not usually a registrar then a local registrar will need to be present at a wedding ceremony.

If the church is not registered then the marriage will take place at a local registry but a religious ceremony can take place at the church afterwards.

Hindu Ceremonies

In a Hindu ceremony, the bride will usually wear a red sari with the groom dressed in white. The ceremony is informal and the guests relax even during the ceremony and chat amongst themselves. As with other marriages, if the building in which the wedding is to take place is registered to hold weddings, couples should give notice of their intention to marry so that a registrar can attend the wedding. If a building is not licensed then a civil ceremony will take place beforehand.

At the actual venue of the wedding, the family of the bride will arrange a sacred place, covered with material and with flowers placed in the centre. The bride will arrive first and will be hidden until the groom and the guests arrive. As the groom enters, lights will be waved over his head and grains of rice are thrown to symbolise wealth and fertility. The groom will then take his place with the bride under the canopy and the ceremony will commence.

Humanist weddings

Humanist weddings eschew religion but generally wish for a wedding ceremony that is fulfilling and emotionally satisfying. Humanists have a national network of trained officers. They have produced a book called *Sharing the Future* which contains details of their approach. It also gives details on sample wedding ceremonies. You can choose to have a ceremony which incorporates your own beliefs without the religious element.

If you contact your local Humanist Association you can locate the nearest officiant. See useful addresses at the end of this book. You may if you wish choose a member of your family or friends to conduct the ceremony, which is simple and straightforward. The main focus is on commitment, love and respect for each other, as it is with all other ceremonies.

A humanist ceremony can take the following form:

- Welcome guests

- Readings by the couple, friends and family about marriage, love and commitment

- Vows made by the couple to each other and children

- Exchange of rings or other tokens

- Readings and poems read by couple and family and friends about their future together

Jewish

In UK civil law, a Jewish marriage may be solemnized in any building, at any time of day, provided the couple have obtained the necessary legal documentation from the registrar. Jewish weddings are solemnized either in an Orthodox synagogue under the authority of the Chief Rabbi, or in a progressive synagogue where the civil authority appoints a marriage secretary who is responsible for the legal side of a ceremony.

For a couple to be able to marry under the Jewish faith both must be Jewish. If one is not Jewish they must undertake a conversion prior to marrying. Jewish weddings usually take place on a Sunday, they cannot be solemnised between sunset on Friday to sunset on Saturday (the Jewish Sabbath).

At the wedding the groom and all males must wear hats and the bride a veil. In all Orthodox and most progressive synagogues the bride must keep her hair covered. Prior to the wedding, the couple may be requested to attend pre-marital counselling with the Rabbi.

The Jewish wedding ceremony

The groom will arrive at the synagogue with his father and best man. When the bride arrives, the groom is escorted under a chuppah (silk or velvet canopy, supported by poles). The bride is led into the synagogue on the arms of her father followed by bridesmaids and the mothers of the couple. The wedding ceremony commences with a blessing from the minister. After the ceremony has ended, the couple are left alone in the synagogue room before joining the festivities. At the reception the Rabbi will say grace in Hebrew before and after the meal, which consists of kosher food. At Orthodox wedding receptions, the men dance around in a big circle between courses, holding handkerchiefs so that they do not touch each other. The bride and groom are carried on chairs around the room. There is lots of singing and dancing.

Muslim weddings
A Muslim bride dresses in a heavily decorated gown, and wears a lot of jewellery. Female guests have their head

and legs covered. Again, as with all other marriages it will be necessary to ensure that all civil requirements are undertaken. This will involve a prior civil ceremony either in a mosque if it is licensed or at a registry office.

Under Muslim beliefs, a marriage is a contract, and not a sacrament, and thus any lay Muslim male may conduct a ceremony. Women are seated on one side of the Mosque with men on the other. The service commences with a sermon and is followed by a reading from the Koran. The bride and groom give their consent to marry and are pronounced man and wife. There are further sermons and prayers and then the party moves onto the bride's house.

 The bride's parents will host a reception, at which guests of the bride bring presents. One week later, the groom's parents host another reception at which the groom's relations and friends bring presents.

Non-conformist weddings

Non-conformist weddings will include Methodist, Baptist, Congregationalist, United-Reform and Assemblies of God faiths. Their services are similar to those offered by the Church of England but they are more flexible and open to innovation. These churches generally need a registrar official to be present at the marriage, as they are not usually registered to conduct marriages.

Pagan ceremonies

Pagan ceremonies encompass New Age Hand-fasting to formal Druid Ceremonies. Pagans are very much nature based and honour equality and unity with nature.

Hand-fasting is an old Anglo-Saxon word for an agreement between two people. The joining of hands is common in many wedding ceremonies. Many other symbols of marriage may be included in the ceremony, such as sharing bread and wine, jumping over a broomstick into a new life together and exchanging rings and tokens. Weddings are generally held out of doors and attended by a Pagan Priest or Priestess.

Druid marriage ceremonies are attended by a druid or druidess. Guests will form a horseshoe, within which the participants at the ceremony will form a circle. 'Four gates' on the four points of the compass divides the circle. Again it is conducted outdoors.

The ceremony involves the celebrants calling on heaven and earth to witness the marriage, before the couple make their vows. The party walk to the four gates, embracing the elements that it represents-fire, water, earth and air. Vows and tokens (rings) are exchanged and a candle is lit. The couple walk around the circle to be greeted by those present as man and wife, before forming a central circle.

Close family and friends make a circle around them and the remaining guests join hands to make a final circle of existence, before a final blessing.

Quaker wedding ceremonies

The Quakers (The Religious Society of Friends) can hold weddings at any time and place. The usual place is the Meeting House normally attended by either or both of the couple. Quaker marriages are a Christian commitment and Quakers, like the Anglican Church, can register their own ceremonies. Like all other marriages, the venue chosen for the ceremony must be licensed, otherwise a civil ceremony will also be required. Marriages where one or both of the couples are divorcees are allowed.

Couples are required to inform their local meeting-house in writing advising of their intention to marry. A meeting is held between the couple and a group of men and women to discuss the forthcoming marriage and its implications.

The service is simple, no procession, music, minister or any other pre-planned element. The couple sit at the front of the Meeting House facing the congregation. The dress is formal but not as elaborate as Anglican wedding ceremonies. Wedding guests can stand and speak at any time. When the bride and groom feel that the time is right to exchange vows they will stand and do so. After they have made their promises, they will return to their seats and the meeting will continue until the elders shake hands to signify that it is over. Rings can be exchanged at any time. Everyone attending the ceremony will go on to the reception.

Single-sex partnerships

The Civil Partnerships Act 2004 sanctioned same sex partnerships giving couples the same rights as heterosexual couples. No religious element is allowed, and the marriage is a civil ceremony conducted in either a registry office or a place licensed to carry out wedding ceremonies. The format of a civil partnerships wedding is exactly the same as that of a heterosexual wedding with slight changes in the wordings of the vows. For more on Civil Partnerships, read A Guide to Civil Partnerships (Emerald Publishing).

Unitarian

Most religious denominations view marriage as a holy sacrament recognised by God. Unitarians view marriage slightly differently as a decision made by two individuals in relation to their own spiritual views and as a freely chosen act rather than a conforming act.

The Unitarian Church welcomes people from different faiths and those who have been previously married. The service itself must contain the legal wording required in all weddings in the UK, the rest of the service is completely individual and may be arranged between you and the officiating minister of that church. You are free to adopt any style that you want. A Unitarian Minister will be able to perform the ceremony at any building registered for solemnization of weddings. The service can be held elsewhere but a civil ceremony must take place first.

The Role of The Best Man

The Reception

6

The Reception

The best man should be among the first to arrive at the reception, along with the bride and groom plus their parents. You should have any messages from people who cannot attend.

Most receptions will have a receiving line. This will normally consist of the brides parents – the hosts –the grooms parents and the bride and groom. The lady in each couple will receive the guests before her partner. If the wedding is very formal, the best man and the chief bridesmaid may join the end of the receiving line. There may also be a toastmaster who will announce the guests as they arrive. At a less formal occasion, the best man may be asked to fill the role of toastmaster.

If either of the couple's parents are divorced the new partners are generally not included in the receiving line.

A drink is generally offered to guests after they have been received. There may be waitresses for this or, if not, the best man and ushers will organise.

A schedule for the reception will already have been worked out beforehand, and therefore the timing of the meal, speeches etc will be known.

The seating arrangements and the meal and speeches

At a set time, the toastmaster will ask their guests to take their seats. If there is no toastmaster, the bride and groom will sit down, which is a signal for the rest of the guests to take their seats. The best man should guide people to their appropriate seats as soon as possible.

The seating plan

The below represents a typical seating plan for a wedding reception

Chief bridesmaid	Grooms father	Bride's mother	Groom	Bride	Brides father	Grooms mother	Best man	Second bridesmaid

This is the conventional seating plan and sometimes it will not be possible to achieve this. It is up to the bride and groom to decide what they want on their big day. A table should be seated to reflect family but also to take into account situations where problems are likely to arise.

One such situation is where both natural and step-parents are present at a wedding. Alternatives can be discussed with the function co-ordinator when booking a wedding.

Below is an alternative plan for where step-parents and natural parents are in attendance.

Best man	Step-mother-groom	Grooms father	Bride's mother	Groom	Bride	Brides father	Grooms mother	Step-father-groom	Chief bridesmaid

This alternative seats all at the top table but puts a healthy distance between the parties.

Wedding speeches

For many people, weddings are the only time in their lives where they will be asked to give a speech. Wedding speeches are most often given by novices who suffer from nerves and self-doubt. However, this is one of the most important days in the life of newly weds and it is crucial that you make a good speech. See the final chapter for more hints on effective speech writing and presentation.

The form

It is usual to have three speeches, and all are toasts. The first toast is proposed by the brides father, or a close family friend or relative. He or she proposes the health of the bride and groom. Next, the groom replies, and proposes a toast to the bridesmaids. Finally, the best man replies on behalf of the bridesmaids.

As with all things, time has changed the usual customs and women are now beginning to assert themselves and make a speech after the groom has finished. Also, best men are also joined by best women.

Each of these speeches need to be prepared in advance and delivered as one would deliver any speech. The following are suggestions for each speech.

The bride and groom

The toast to the bride and groom should express happiness at the occasion and wish them both luck in their new life. It is customary to compliment the bride on her appearance and to compliment the groom on his luck. You may wish to add an anecdote from having known the bride so long, or you may have a funny story about the first time you met the groom. Finish by asking the guests to raise their glasses and drink to the health of the bride and groom.

The things not to do at a wedding speech

- Never make jokes about the bride or mother in law. This is pathetic and outdated

- Never make remarks which are in bad taste

- Avoid smut, innuendo or references to past partners

- Don't use the opportunity to score points

- Keep in mind that this is the bride and grooms special day, so only add to their pleasure.

The groom

Next up is the groom, who thanks the proposer of the previous toast and in turn proposes the toast to the bridesmaids. The groom usually compliments the bride on her appearance and thanks her for consenting to marry him. He usually compliments on his good fortune on having found her. He thanks his best man for supporting him, and for working so hard to ensure that the day has run so smoothly.

Sometimes, the groom also thanks the bride's family for allowing him the honour of marrying her. However, this is increasingly seen as sexist and outdated. The groom, however, should at least thank the bride's family for accepting him in their home.

The groom then proceeds to tell a few anecdotes before he turns to the subject of the bridesmaids. He should compliment them on how well turned out they are and thank them for attending his wife so well. He will finish by proposing a toast to the bridesmaids.

The main event

The best man's speech is usually the highlight of the wedding. The audience is expected to laugh and the speech is usually timed at between five to ten minutes.

Start by thanking the groom on behalf of the bridesmaids. Add your compliments to both them and the bride.
The usual course of events after this is to say something about your relationship with the groom, and to recount some lively stories about your youth together. If you did not know each other when you were younger then tell a few stories about recent events. While it is expected that you will embarrass the groom slightly, it is important that you do not overstep the mark and ruin his reputation.

Best man's humour

You should not allow your speech to turn into a string of jokes, just for the sake of getting laughs. Never make jokes in bad taste and keep in mind the age and profile of those present. Avoid lewd comments. At the end of your speech, read any telegrams or other communications of good wishes, and introduce any special guests. Keep this section short, as the audience might become restless.

Other speeches

If the bride and groom take a decision to vary this format,

they should tell everyone involved and work out who is going to propose which toast.

If the bride wishes to make a speech, she usually takes the opportunity to propose the toast to the people who have made the wedding such a special occasion.

While you are quite at liberty to arrange for as many speeches as you wish, avoid allowing them to go on for too long. It is highly likely that alcohol, food, endless speeches and so on, will all have taken their toll.

Cutting the cake

The last part of the ceremony is cutting the wedding cake. After the speeches the best man (or toastmaster) announces that the cake is to be cut by the bride and groom. The couple will hold the knife over the cake and together make the first symbolic cut. If the cake is large enough, it is tradition for the top tier to be saved for later, for example for the first wedding anniversary or christening.

Display of gifts

It is traditional to display gifts at the bride's parents home. However, a display can be arranged at the reception so that all the guests can view them. Each gift on display should have a name tag attached and should be arranged in order of what they are, i.e. crockery and so on. After the reception, the bride's mother should pack away all the gifts and store then safely until they can be delivered to the newlywed's home.

Final Duties

Once the wedding day is over, there is very little else for the best man to do. If the suits were hired, make sure that your suit and the groom's suit are returned in good time. Remind the ushers to return their suits as well.

7

More Hints on Speechwriting and Presentation

Because the idea of making a speech is usually very nerve wracking for many people, the following tips are essential if you want to make a real impact with the best man's speech.

Public speaking generally

Before looking at the crafting of a speech, we need to look at public speaking generally. It is only when you learn the art of public speaking that you can become an accomplished speaker and, by definition, deliver an effective speech. It is very much more than just standing up and talking to others, as you will probably have started to gather.

Public speaking is very much an art and a skill which can be mastered by anyone. It is true to say that some people may be initially better equipped for the role of public speaker than others, by virtue of their own particular personality type. However, the truly effective public speaker learns the craft and applies certain techniques which generally derive from experience.

The person and the material

There are two vital ingredients in public speaking. The first is very much the person delivering the speech or other material to a group. The second is the nature of the material being delivered.

The Person

For some people, standing in front of an audience, whatever the size, is not a real problem. For others however, the very thought of exposing one-self to a group of people, and being so vulnerable, is a nightmare best avoided.

When trying to put this into context it is important to remember that, when we communicate as part of a group, or simply on a one to one basis with another, then we interact primarily through speech and body language. We are often confident within ourselves because we feel secure in that we are part of a group interacting and that all eyes are not on us alone, at least not for a protracted period.

The situation is very different indeed when we are alone and faced with a group of people, strangers or not, and we have to present material. It means that we have to assume responsibility and take the lead and communicate successfully to others. Nervousness is very often the result when placed in this situation because, until we can make contact with the audience and establish a rapport, we are very much alone and feel vulnerable.

Obviously, there are a number of factors influencing the levels of confidence and differences in attitude between people, such as the nature and type of the person and their background, their past experience, both within the family and in the world of work and numerous other experiences besides. All these will affect a persons ability to become an effective public speaker.

Why do we feel nervous?

There are a number of reasons why we may feel nervous. You need to question yourself and ask yourself why. Was the sight of so many faces in front of you enough to frighten you and make you lose your self confidence or are you plagued by the memory of previous mistakes? You need to remember that you change and develop as a person as you gain more experience and that past mistakes do not mean that you will repeat them.

Lets face it, most of us will experience nerves in a situation which is stressful to us. This is totally normal and quite often we become anxious and charged with adrenaline which drives us on. When it comes to speaking in public the adrenaline can be positive but excessive nerves are negative and can lead to aggression.

Fundamentally, the key to successful public speaking is the acquisition of confidence coupled with assertiveness which leads to the ability to effectively control a situation. If you are assertive and you know your subject matter you are likely to be confident and in control and less likely to feel nervous.

Be prepared!

Directly related to the above, preparation is everything and to feel confident with your material means that you are half way there already.

You should listen to speakers, particularly good speakers as often as possible in order to gain tips. Notice the way that good and effective speakers construct their sentences. Listen for the eloquence. Remember, shorter sentences have a lot more impact and are easier to grasp than long sentences. They also act a discipline for the speaker in that they will prevent him or her from straying off the point.

Another very important tip when approaching the day of your presentation is preparing yourself psychologically.

Convince yourself that you are looking forward to the speech and that you will do well no matter what. Convey this to your audience as you open your presentation, say that you are glad to be with them and that you hope that this goes well for all. This reinforces a feeling of goodwill and will express itself through your body language and your voice.

Finally, one of the main aids to effective public speaking is *experience* and that only comes through practice so it is essential that you take every opportunity offered you to sharpen your skills in this area.

Structuring a speech

A good speech is pieced together in a defined structure and contains a number of specific elements. The structure of a speech should comprise the following:

- The opening. This is where the speaker needs to grab the attention of the audience

- Introduction to the subject. This is where the speaker gives an overview of the material to be covered

- The body of the speech. This is where the speaker presents information or arguments

- Close. This is where the speaker draws conclusions

from the information already presented and leaves the audience with something to think about.

Although most compositions have a beginning, middle and end speeches can differ somewhat. The most important difference between a speech and other presentations is that a speech is fleeting, it is uttered and then disappears. It is not possible for a listener of a speech to go back to the beginning if they are not paying attention. At least not during the speech, maybe after with a transcript. The good speech writer will therefore build in elements so that the audience is kept alert. These elements are:

- Splashes. These are attention grabbers which surprise people and gain their interest right at the beginning

- Appeals. These are where sentences identify the speakers purpose with the needs of the audience

- Links. These are sentences that link one piece of argument to the next in a logical manner.

It is easier to write the introduction and main body of your speech before you tackle the opening and the close. You will write a more effective opening and close if you deal with them together at the end of the writing process.

- Summaries and repetitions. These are useful techniques to ensure that the audience follows the argument and remembers as much as possible after you have stepped out of the limelight. The general rule is: tell them what you are going to tell them; tell them; and then tell them what you have told them.

Openings

When a speaker starts to speak, or rises to begin to speak, the audience will appraise him or her on the physical appearance. The second critical moment is when the first words are uttered. Apart from the formal address, the elements to build into the opening are: a splash, an appeal and credentials, followed by a statement of the topic on which you are going to speak. The splash is a method of grabbing the audience's attention. Choose a splash that is relevant and also topical. Once the audience is paying attention, make them see that your topic is not only interesting, but also relevant to their experience and needs.

Next, prove to the audience that you are someone who has something interesting and worthwhile to say, and that your facts can be relied upon. State your credentials, then give a short sharp simple explanation of what it is that you are going to talk about, and what you hope to achieve by doing so. These last two elements, the statement of your subject and your objectives should be, in effect, a promise to go some way towards fulfilling the audiences needs.

A strong opening should be confident, friendly, short and simple. The speaker who apologizes or who undermines his/herself will lose respect immediately. On the other hand, a long rambling opening will confuse and irritate, boding no good for the rest of the speech.

Introduction

When you have completed the arrangement of the material, you should have a series of headings that lead from one another logically. Under each of these headings you will have a number of pieces of material to utilize. During the introduction, you need to set out for the audience the main elements of your argument. State each of the headings in the order in which you are going to present them, and explain what they mean. Tell the audience what it is that you are going to tell them.

Closing a speech

It is a fact that most audiences have a very short time span. They are generally attentive at the start of a presentation, but after a few minutes their concentration begins to waver. However, they will usually perk up again towards the end of the speech. The close of the speech is just as important as the opening and it is up to the speaker to make sure that the audience attention is held. The close should be a short summary of all the material that you covered in your presentation, and you should draw any conclusion from the arguments that you have presented. In this way you will repeat the salient points that you wished to put across, and the audience is likely to remember some of what you have said.

Always end on a high note and try to leave the audience with words that sum up your speech. Above all, make sure that you close confidently and that your audience know that the speech is over. Avoid at all cost the pregnant pause or the embarrassed silence.

Presentation skills

Having looked at preparation for speech writing and also structuring a speech, it is now necessary to consider some more specific points connected with presentation of a speech.

Personal skills

Body Language

People have a natural ability to use body language together with speech. Body language emphasises speech and enables us to communicate more effectively with others. It is vitally important when preparing for the role of public speaker to understand the nature of your body language and also to connect this to another all important element-*vision*.

Vision

People tend to take in a lot of information with their eyes and obviously presentations are greatly enhanced by use of visual aids. Together, when presenting to a group of people, as a public speaker, *body language and visual stimuli* are all important. A great amount of thought needs to go into the elements of what it is that you are about to present and the way you intend to convey your message. What you should not do, especially as a novice, is to stand up in front of a group and deliver a presentation off the top of your head. You need to carry out thorough research into what it is you are presenting and to whom you are presenting.

Developing a style

Every person engaged in public speaking will have his or her own style. At the one end of the spectrum there are those people who give no thought to what it is they are doing and have no real interest in the audience. For them it is a chore and one which should be gotten over as soon as is possible. Such public speakers can be slow, boring and ineffectual leaving only traces of annoyance in the audiences mind. Here, there is a definite absence of style.

At the other end of the spectrum are those who have given a great deal of thought to what they are doing, given a great deal of thought to their material and have a genuine interest in the audience. Such public speakers will be greatly stimulating and leave a lasting impression and actually convey something of some worth.

It does not matter what the occasion of your public speaking role is, wedding (best mans speech etc.) seminar, presentation to employers. The principles are the same-that is understanding your material, understand the nature of yourself as you relate to the material and how this will translate into spoken and body language and also how you will use visual aids to enhance the presentation.

Underlying all of this is your *own personal style,* partly which develops from an understanding of the above and partly from an understanding of yourself. Some presenters of material recognise their own speed of presentation, i.e. slow, medium or fast and also understand their own body language. Some are more fluent than others, use their hands more etc. Having recognized your own style what you need to do is to adjust your own way of presentation to the specific requirements of the occasion. The key point is to gain attention, get the message across and be stimulating to a degree. Obviously some occasions are more formal than others. You should study the nature of the occasion and give a lot of thought to what is required, i.e. degree of humor, seriousness etc. All of the above considerations begin to translate themselves into a style which you yourself will begin to recognize and feel comfortable with. Once this occurs you will find that, when presenting, your nerves will begin to melt away and your confidence begins to develop

Use of language

The use of language is a specific medium which must be understood when making a presentation. Obviously, if you are speaking publicly to a group of familiar people who know and understand you, a different approach will be needed and a different form of language, perhaps less formal, utilized than that used in front of a group who are totally unfamiliar.

Nevertheless, using formal but simple language interspersed with funny remarks is undoubtedly one of the best ways to approach any form of audience, friends or not. You should certainly avoid too much detail and do not go overboard with funny comments as this will become tedious. Stick to the subject matter lightening up the occasion with a few anecdotes and witty comments. It is all about the right blend and pitch.

Body Language

We have briefly discussed body language. It is astounding how much you can tell about people in the street by simply observing their body language. Usually people form an impression about another within the first five minutes of meeting. It is essential, in a public speaking situation that your body language should reflect a confident personality with a good sense of humor. In order to achieve this you should think about the following:

Use of hands

- Use your hands to emphasize what you say and to invite the audience to accept your point

- Keep your hands open and keep your fingers open.

- Avoid putting your hands in your pocket and avoid closing them. Firmly avoid pointing fingers

- Co-ordinate your hand movements with your words.

Using facial expressions

People tend to concentrate on the face of a public speaker, in addition to the movements of the body. Obviously, your face, along with body language is a vehicle for expression. A smile every now and again is important. There are other actions which can help:

- Use of eyebrows for inviting people to accept your ideas
- Moving the head to look at all members of a group. Very important indeed to maintain a sense of involvement on the part of all
- Do not fix your eyes on one place or person for long. This will isolate the rest of the audience and may be interpreted as nervousness or a lack of confidence on your part
- Look at individuals every time you mention something in their area of expertise or are singling them out in a positive way
- Look at people even if they appear not to be looking at you

The face is a very important part of the communication apparatus and the use of this part of the body is of the utmost importance when public speaking.

Controlling your movements

In addition to the use of face and hands the way you move can have an effect on your audience. Your movements can vary from standing rigid and fixed to acting out roles and being fluid generally. There are, in.

keeping with body language generally, certain rules relating to movement:

- Restrict your movements only to those which are most necessary. Avoid throwing yourself all over the place and distracting peoples attention from the emphasis of your presentation

- Always face the people that you are addressing. Never look at the floor or away from the audience, at least not for a prolonged period of time

Practicing presentations

Taking into account all of the above and then practicing. This is the absolute key to successful presentations and to effective public speaking. Practice most certainly lifts your confidence level up and assists you in staying in control The more time and effort that you spend practicing the less that you will have to worry about when presenting. Lets face it, a presentation is a live stage show. How do stand up comics feel when they expose themselves to an audience? Develop a practicing technique by trying different methods:

- You should choose a topic that you are very interested in and prepare a short presentation on it.
- Stand in front of a mirror and present to yourself. Repeat this over and over, observing different aspects of your style.

- Try to rectify any bad habits.

- Experiment with various styles and techniques until you find one that suits you.

- Try to film yourself if possible. Replay the film and observe yourself. This is one of the most effective ways of changing your style, or developing your style.

- Ask a friend to observe you and to make detailed criticism. Do not be afraid of criticism as this is always constructive

At this point you should be concentrating on style only. Do not worry about content as we will be discussing this a little later.

Developing your voice

It is perfectly possible, and probably essential to improve on four characteristics of your speech:

- tone

- pitch

- volume

- clarity.

Tone

If you restrict your body cavities responsible for amplifying sound, your voice will sound restricted and sometimes nasal. Restriction of body cavities can happen by standing or sitting in the wrong way.

It is essential that you give thought to your posture and bearing when public speaking.

Pitch

As you stretch and loosen your voice chords, the pitch of your voice will change. When stretched, the number of vibrations increases due to the small distance allowed for them to vibrate. These vibrations produce high frequency (pitch) sounds. When the vocal chords are loose, more distance is allowed for them to vibrate which makes them produce low frequency (pitch) sounds.

Volume

The volume of your voice can be improved in two ways. The first is by simply increasing the pressure of air coming out of your lungs, or by narrowing the space between the vocal chords (glottis). You can change the volume of a whisper simply by increasing the amount of air through your glottis which is widely open. Try to shout. You will notice that your glottis contracts sharply, to increase the volume of your voice.

Clarity

To get your message across you need to say it clearly. Clarity is determined by the speech organs and how well you can control them. If you are too nervous your tongue and lips start playing tricks on you because they are tense. In order to speak clearly, overcome the problems associated with speech organs and get your message across. Don't be scared of moving your lips. Exercise your speech muscles. Make sure that you pronounce things clearly and that you carry your voice.

Voice pitch

People generally feel more comfortable listening to a deep voice, one that is well rounded and smooth. However, it is important to ensure that your voice is at your natural pitch and not forced. To find your natural pitch, concentrate on the following exercises:

- Speak at the lowest note that feels comfortable to you

- Use a musical instrument, e.g. a guitar or piano and find the note that corresponds to your lowest comfortable pitch

- Move four notes up the musical scale. This should be very close to your natural pitch

- Try to tune your voice with this note and speak with the music helping you to stay in tune
- Practice this as many times as you need, in order to become confident in finding your natural pitch quite quickly.

When you have found the natural pitch of your voice, you will need to work on some variations to make your speech more natural. Changing the pitch up and down according to the contents of the speech helps you to keep the audience attracted to what you are saying. Try saying a few sentences out loud and practice varying the pitch. You can then notice the relation between the contents of the sentences and your pitch when saying each of them. When you realize what you are capable of achieving with your voice, you can then consciously start varying the pitch. Singing is very good for voice training and realizing the potential of your voice organs. Reading out loud and trying to act a story is also good training.

Voice projection
Voice projection depends on two main factors:

- Physical

- Psychological

The physical factor comprises

- The force with which you breathe

- The muscular power you put into forming the words

- The clarity of your pronunciation

If you get all these factors right then you will have no problem in projecting your voice. However, some people feel nervous in front of an audience and they fail to project their voice properly. In a lot of cases, speakers project their voices too much or too little simply because they do not look at the audience and estimate the power that they need to project. In order to estimate projection, you should look at the person the furthest away from you and imagine that you are talking too him or her. You will feel the need to project your voice to that person and be able to control your vocal organs and breathing accordingly.

Use of the body

To help you to project your voice, you should make use of the resonance of your body cavities. Try the following:

- Relax the muscles in your neck and stand comfortably without bending or over straightening your chest.

- Also relax the muscles in your neck by nodding gently a few times.

- Take a deep breath and exhale, letting out a deep sound. You can then realize how the cavity in your chest resonates giving out a sigh of relief.

The nose
A clear nose helps you to speak clearly and project your voice. If your nose is blocked, it is harder for you to pronounce certain letters let alone project your voice. It is also easier to breathe through a clear nose and therefore maintain the breathing rhythm.

Appendix 1 Wedding Planner and Monthly/weekly/daily diary

The first outline planner should be completed on the request for you to be best man. This will give you an overview of the whole proceedings and enable you to gain a clear picture and keep control right from the outset. The ongoing diary acts as a countdown to the wedding and will help you in the ongoing planning.

1. Wedding planner

Date of the wedding..

The Wedding Party

Bride's name..

Address..

Phone number..

email..

Mobile..

Groom's name..

Address..

Phone.............................. Mobile ....

E-mail..
Chief Bridesmaid's name..

Address..

Phone.............................. Mobile.......................

E-Mail..

Other bridesmaid's names and ages (if children)

....

....

....

....

Bride's parent's names..

Address..

Phone.............................. Mobile ....

E-mail..

Groom's parents names.......................................
Address...

Phone................................. mobile.....................

E-mail...

Chief usher's name...

Address...

Phone................................... Mobile.............

Usher's name..

Address...

Phone...

E-Mail...

Usher's name..

Address...

Phone...

E-Mail...

Clothing

Colour scheme for bride and
bridesmaid's..
....

Formal wear or suit required (tick)
Accessories required (tick)

Transport

Groom and best man to church (tick)
Bridesmaids to reception (tick)
Parents to reception (tick)
Guests to reception (tick)
Bride and groom for honeymoon (tick)

The ceremony

Time...
Venue...
Name of minister/registrar....................................
Phone...
Rehearsal date and time.......................................
Arrival time for groom and best man.........................
Fees to organist...
Order of service sheets..
Ushers duties..
Buttonholes/corsages...

Photograph arrangements.......................................
Parking facilities..

The reception

Time...
Venue..
Contact..
Phone..
E-mail...
Parking facilities...
Number of guests...
Guests to be announced...
Toastmaster..
Receiving line...
Seating plan...
Meal arrangements and times....................................
Bar facilities...
Timing of speeches...
People to thank in speech......................................
Music/entertainment..
Present display..
Changing room for bride and groom..............................
Leaving time...
Departure details..

Other details..

....

....

....

....

....

2. Monthly/weekly/daily planner

6 months before wedding

Confirm acceptance with groom (tick)
Book wedding date in diary (tick)
Cancel any other arrangements (tick)

3 months before wedding

Discuss wedding plans with bride and groom (tick)
Help to choose the ushers (tick)
Help with the wedding preparations (tick)

2 months to go

Consult the wedding gift list and decide on present (tick)
Arrange to pay for and fit your own outfit (tick)
Check that groom and ushers have organised their known outfits (tick)
Prepare and draft speech (tick)
Compile a list of close family (tick)
Visit reception venue with bride and groom to check all details (tick)

Remind groom to check passports, order currency, get inoculations etc (tick)

6 weeks to go

Organise stag party (tick)
Book venue for stag party (tick)
Check licence/banns arrangements have been made
 (tick)

1 month to go

Check buttonholes have been ordered (tick)
Check honeymoon arrangements have been made (tick)
Check route to grooms home, church etc by carrying out
test run (tick)
Arrange transport for groom and self to church, reception
and home (tick)
Arrange going away vehicle for newlyweds (tick)
Arrange own transport from reception (tick)
Arrange car service if appropriate (tick)
Buy decorations for going away car (tick)

2 weeks to go
Finalise speech (tick)
Check parking arrangements at church/reception (tick)
1 week to go

Attend wedding rehearsal (tick)
Fill in wedding day schedule (tick)
Hand over gift to bride and groom (tick)
Check rings are purchased (tick)

Check licence/banns certificate is collected (tick)
Collect order of service sheets (tick)

2 days to go

Check and confirm transport arrangements (tick)

1 day to go

Collect hired suit (tick)
Check accessories (tick)
Check buttonholes (tick)
Check car (tick)
Ensure going away luggage is packed (tick)
Book alarm call if necessary (tick)

Good Luck-its all in the planning!

Useful addresses
Addresses for copies of documents such as birth certificates etc.

General Register Office for England and Wales
Family Records Office
Smedley Hydro
Trafalgar Road
Birkdale
Southport
Merseyside
PR8 2HH

Tel: 01704 569824

The Registrar general for England and Wales
Office of Population, Census and Surveys
St Catherine's House
10 Kingsway
London WC2B 6JP

Tel: 0207 242 0262

General Register Office for Northern Ireland
Oxford House
49-55 Chichester Street
Belfast BT1 4HL

01232 235211

General Register Office for Scotland
New Register House
Edinburgh
EH1 3YT

Tel: 0131 334 0380

General Register office for the Isle of Man
Finch Road
Douglas
Isle of Man

Tel: 01624 5212

Registrar General for Guernsey
The Greffe
Royal Court House
St Peter Port
Guernsey

Tel: 01481 725277

Addresses for civil and religious ceremony information.

Catholic wedding ceremonies
Catholic Marriage Advisory Council
Clitheroe House
1 Blythe Mews

Blythe Road
London W14 ONW

Celtic ministers

The Pagan Federation
Box 7097
London SW1N 3XX

Foreign and Commonwealth Office

The Nationality Treaty and Claims Department
Clive House
Petty France
London SW1H 9HD

Tel: 0207 238 4567

Humanist ceremonies

British Humanist Association
47 Theobald's Road
London W1X 8SP

Jewish ceremonies

Jewish Marriage Council
23 Ravenshurst Avenue
London NW4 4EE

Union of Liberal and Progressive Synagogues
The Montagu Centre
21 Mapel Street
London W1P 7DS

Office for Overseas Marriage Enquiries

General Register Office
Overseas Section
Smedley Hydro
Trafalgar Road
Southport PR8 2HH

Quaker ceremonies

Quakers (The religious Society of Friends)
Friends House
173-177 Euston Road
London Nw1 2BJ

Scottish Weddings

Church of Scotland
121 George Street
Edinburgh EH2 4YN

Single-sex unions

Lesbian and Gay Christian Movement
Oxford House
Derbyshire Street
London E2 6HG

Unitarian ceremonies

Unitarian Church
Essex Hall
1-6 Essex Street
London WC2R 3HY

Other addresses

Family planning

The British Pregnancy Advisory Service
Austy manor
Wootton Wawen
Solihull
West Midlands B95 6BX

The Brook Advisory Centre
153a East Street
London SE17 2SD 0207 703 7880

Catholic Marriage Care
Clitheroe House
1 Blythe Mews
Blythe Road
London W14 ONW

Tel: 0207 371 1341

The Family Planning Association
2-12 Pentonville Road
London N1 9FP

Tel: 0207 837 5432

Scottish Catholic Marriage care
196 Clyde Street
Glasgow
G1 4JY

Honeymoon
The Association of British Travel Agents
55-57 Newman Street
London W1 4AH
Tel: 0207 393 2000

Information Services

National Wedding Information Service
National House

Freepost 121-123 High Street
Epping
CM16 4BD

Tel: Freephone 0800 009027

Photography

The Association of Photographers
9-10 Domingo Street
London
EC1 OTA

Tel: 0207 608 1441

The Guild of Wedding Photographers
13 Market Street
Altrincham
Cheshire
WAS14 1QS

0161 926 9367

Index

Anglican ceremonies 54
Anglican church 19
Annulled marriages 16
Assisting the bridegroom 45

Banns 19
Blessing ceremonies 58
Buddhist weddings 58
Buttonholes 46

Catholic weddings 59
Choosing the ushers 49
Christian Scientist Church 61
Church of England 19
Civil Ceremonies 22
Common licence 20
Common parenthood 25
Corsages 46
Cutting the cake 78

Day of the wedding 52
Display of gifts 78
Divorced persons 21
Duty to live together 24
Duty to maintain 24

Effects of a marriage 24
Engagement 17

Fidelity 24
Final duties 80

Grounds for annulment 16

Hindu ceremonies 61
Hiring a suit 48
Humanist weddings 62

Jewish weddings 63
Joint assets 25

Licence to marry 19
Lounge suits 47

Marriage Act 1983 22
Marriages abroad 23
Marriage (Registrar General's Licence) Act 1970 22
Marriage and cohabitation 14
Marital confidences 25
Marriages of convenience 26
Marriage formalities 18
Morning dress 47
Muslim weddings 64

Non-conformist weddings 65

Order of service sheets 46
Organising a stag party 39
Organising wedding clothes 47

Pagan ceremonies 66
Practical jokes 41
Public speaking 81

Quaker weddings 67
Qualities of a best man 31

Reception 35 72
Religious ceremonies 18
Role of best man 31
Role of the ushers 48

Seating plans 51 73
Sexual relationships 24
Single-sex partnerships 68
Special licence 20
Speeches 74
Superintendent registrars certificate 20
Surnames 25

The ceremony 54
The wedding 44

Unitarian weddings 68

Void marriages 16
Voidable marriages 16
Voluntary marriages 15

Witnesses 23